Where The Heart Is

poetry *Pt* today

WHERE THE HEART IS

Edited by
Kelly Olsen

First published in Great Britain in 1998 by Poetry
Today, an imprint of
Penhaligon Page Ltd, 12 Godric Square, Maxwell Road,
Peterborough. PE2 7JJ

A Catalogue record for this book is available from the
British Library.

ISBN 1 86226 083 4

Typesetting and layout, Penhaligon Page Ltd, England.
Printed and bound by Forward Press Ltd, England

Foreword

Where The Heart Is is a compilation of poetry, featuring some of our finest poets. The book gives an insight into the essence of modern living and deals with the reality of life today. We think we have created an anthology with a universal appeal.

There are many technical aspects to the writing of poetry and *Where The Heart Is* contains free verse and examples of more structured work from a wealth of talented poets. To choose winners from the wide range of styles and forms is a most difficult task, albeit a pleasurable one. I have tried to choose a variety, to represent the poetry of today so the winners are:

J Bowen	Nature's Style
L Allen	Swansea Locked On . . .!
S Murgatroyd	Step Back In Time
A Slattery	Isles Of Beauty
A Moore	Filey Brigg

My congratulations and thanks go to them and to all of you who have contributed to *Where The Heart Is*, and I trust you will enjoy it as much as I have.

Contents

Rocking Chair
Elisabeth Dill Perrin

I can always picture her there,
sitting alone in the room.
Always in her rocking chair,
no other chair would do.
How could she feel so happy,
we would often ask ourselves.
When nothing could she see,
and never would it be.
But always quite content,
with so much on her mind.
Knowing we were always near,
meant everything to her.
Well! she was such a special dear.
Now! each time I gaze at that rocking chair,
my heart remembers still,
the many hour's she sat alone.
With her thought's her memories too,
always in her rocking chair,
no other chair would do.

Shropshire
John Blesson

Dawn breaks on a sleepy valley,
The mist is swirling through the trees,
Cattle grazing in the meadows,
Standing in a gentle breeze.
The sun is still a watery yellow,
Its rays are not yet warm,
The footpath's still a little muddy,
After last night's summer storm.

That's the way it has been here ever
Ever since the dawn of time,
We would never try to change it,
O How we love this tranquil shrine,
England here in all its glory,
Everywhere is lush and green,
A church spire showing through the tree tops,
Just the ways it's always been.

If this place could tell its story,
What a tale it could tell,
Of the battles, of the glories,
Of the knights who fought and fell,
Of the sickness and the famine,
All have happened through the years,
Of the joys and of the laughter,
Of the hurts and of the tears.

As time passed on right throughout the centuries,
Saxon, Norman, cavalier, Roundheads,
With all their reformation.
All in turn have passed through here,
Romans built the roads and bridges,
They have stood the test of time,
So let us not destroy this hub of history,
This sacred land divine.

Home

J Jackson

This dear old house I'm living in
Is where I care to roam,
With memories of my bygone years
It's the place that I call home.

I wander in the garden
Among the scented flowers,
I cross over to the apple tree
Where I'd swing for hours & hours.

The old car's standing in the drive
My cat lies in the sun
My faithful dog trots by my side
Together we have fun.

Now everyone's home is his castle
How ever meagre of small
It's where you find love & laughter
With your children, as I recall,

It's where everyone has a birthday
And parties, there'll surely be
Then Xmas brings us gifts galore
With a wonderful Xmas tree.

Then as we tend our gardens
Toiling ready for the spring
With daffodils and tulips
The birds begin to sing.

Now with summer in the garden
We sit with peace of mind.
There's butterflies & honey bees
God's gift to all mankind.

Leadhills
Margaret M Osoba

Ah, good, I'm very glad to see
The spirit of community
In Leadhills where I used to stay
Is still alive and well today.

For there, some sixty years ago
The pace of life was calm and slow.
In winter's storms and summer sun,
'Twas 'each for all, and all for one'.

Snowed up we were in wintertime,
But still we took it in our stride.
Though sometimes stuck, our little train,
The snowplough cleared the rails again.

No TV then to tell our tale
Of high endeavour, hill and vale.
We helped each other, old and young,
And just said, 'Keep on keeping on!'

Floating Free
P J Littlefield

My special place, would have to be,
Up in my spacecraft, floating free,
I could watch from on high,
The human race passing by,
I would feel no envy or greed,
No assets or trappings would I need,
Jealously and anguish, were mine no more,
Anger and pain were shown the door,
I could view the Earth from afar,
A jewel set in space, shining like a star,
I'd see night come, as day ebbed by,
Them to America I'd up and fly,
As a treat I'd swoop down to Everest's lea,
Then touch down on Table Top Mountain for my tea,
Then off again I would soar,
To China's wall and so much more,
And if an impending disaster I did spy,
I'd be down to help, in the blink of an eye,
Sat one morning contemplating my lot,
In a hollow close to Ayers Rock,
Loneliness sneaked up and nudged my mind,
My thoughts turned to the lady and love I left behind,
I decided then and there, that after three whole years
I couldn't float free for eternity,
So I aimed my craft for my home town of Wetherby,
Some time later, I touched down on the green,
People came out in their hundreds to the scene,

The police and media were out in force,
And the Salvation Army were their of course,
I clambered out and the people cheered and the children
waved,
As if I was a hero or a film star or the world had
saved,
And then my lady came and held me close,
I knew then, that this was the special place I needed
most.

Waterfall
Maxine Bassett (11)

Reflective water trickles off stony rocks, above
my waterfall,
I sit behind it, drizzles melt into my pot,
for raspberry jam I make.
Smelly plants of rich bright colours,
put me to fantasy dreams,
this is my special place.
A big blue sky, fades away,
dawn is long gone,
the night comes to play.
I wish I could have stayed there,
the sun beating down on me,
the water, jam, dreams, & sun,
made me feel protected, loved, cared &
free,
I hope it is now a secret,
kept for me again to see.

Going Back
Doreen Turner

I returned to that perfect place
For that is how I remembered it.
The excitement if buying my ticket
And boarding the train.

The little station looked shabby
No flowers this time
I hurried through the barrier
Towards the winding lane.

When the cottage came into sight
The place of happy memories
I saw a scruffy little shack
I wished at once I had not gone back.

Keep in your heart your dearest thoughts
Of moments and places you've loved.
Don't try to recapture, never try to reclaim
Nothing is ever the same.

Cavalese
Mary Williams

Into the valley of death . . .
Swooped the fighter plane.
Having a bit of harmless fun.
What's wrong with that?

Everything.
These were not the enemy
These in the cable car
In their bright ski gear.

(If they'd known before
They'd have come fitter dressed
To meet their end.
In funeral suits perhaps).

Anyway, *their* fun was over
In mid-air, you might say
No time to say goodbye,
Even to a near neighbour.

'I DID it. Did you see that?
I flew lower than anyone has.
Just feet from the ground -
It has to be a record'.

It was a record for sure
And one that will stand.
Who wants *more* than 20 lives
Tumbled out red on the snow?

And the plane? 'Look Bill,
There's a spot of damage
On the tail. What caused that,
I wonder?' Well you might.

You severed the cable
With the tail of your plane.
That's what. Cut it fast
Like an umbilical cord.

Only death, not life resulted.
How's that for a record?

Cavalese - an Italian ski resort where 20 people died when a US
military jet sliced through the cable and the cab plunged to the
ground. 4/2/98

My Childhood
Lucy Wilson

When I was a child on my father's farm
I often wonder how I never came to harm
Early morning we would milk the cows
Then feed the horses and the sows.

Milk to deliver to customers doors
Then back home to swill byre floors
Two shire horses to harness now
Off to the fields to harrow and plough

Potatoes all planted and harvested
By hand
From dawn until dark we tilled the land
No combine harvester to reap the corn
A horse drawn binder that was all
The sheaves of corn stocked to dry
This is how my childhood days went by

Long and dark were the nights
Without TV or electric lights
German bombers overhead
I was always dragged out of bed
Down into air-raid shelters
So dark and damp
I awoke in the morning cold and cramped

I wonder what children would
Do today
If they had to work and live this way

Our Friend The Romany
Mary Hoyle

Mark my son he opened the door
A Romany-A gypsy he saw
His eyes were wide as she read his palm
It's okay Mark I will tell you no harm
He came away with his face aglow
A piece of lace for him to show
The 'Gypsy' had told him what he wanted
                                to know
The lady of the house whose palm she read
Mark's mum of course I should have said
Took her lace & wished no harm.
'The special wishes that you gave
Are only for Mark & me to save'.
            God bless you on your way
We hope to meet again someday.

The Best Dad
Nicola Reid (10)

My dad's the best dad,
He isn't really very bad.
I don't know if he like kippers,
But I know he's got smelly slippers.
My dad's the best,
Even though he wears a woolly vest/
He's not got a rash,
But he talks a lot of trash.
My dad's great,
But he's usually late.
Some people say he's as thin as a line,
But I don't care because he's mine.

My Grandchild
Terry Astwood

On the day that, he was born
Four magpies on the fence
Could this be a turn of fate
Or just coincidence.

Just before the witching hour
As midnight fast drew near
A lovely new born baby boy
Was beginning to appear

A healthy five pounds six he weighed
Which brought to all a smile
In incubator he was put
But only for a while

Setting out on life's rich trail
Who knows what will unfold
Such hopes I dream of for this boy
As in my arms I hold.

I wonder if those magpies knew
Sat upon the fence
Could this be a turn of fate
Or just coincidence.

My Special Place
Joe Bayford

My special place,
Is far away,
A long journey,
Takes all day.

A train or coach
To start, I'll need.
Then a ferry,
Calm sea, and God speed.

My destination,
Is now in sight
You've probably guessed.
It's the Isle of Wight.

For Your Eyes Alone
C Wilson

Some eyes say a lot, others do not,
One lies while another one cries,
Some speak with money, others are funny
Most people speak with their eyes.
How ever well meant with good intent
To a brown eyed blonde of Italian descent
This old fool does apologise,
That smile of yours could open doors,
Few people smile with their eyes.
Keep smiling please
While I lay off the many years.

The Dig
H M Liebeschuetz

This is the foreman's country. To him I'm a guest,
Working for him and his people, not lining my nest.
The foreman is watching me closely. What have I done wrong?
A moment ago he was whistling a cheerful small song.

Now he stands at my elbow intently, all senses alert
What treasure beneath us is hidden in this patch of dirt?
Is it archaeological, ancient, some centuries old?
Will it glitter with silver and jewels or just gleam with gold?

Now he has started probing. The treasure's in sight.
He holds it in triumph before me and then he takes flight.
My stint in his country is over. I've finished my term.
The foreman is our garden robin, the treasure - a worm!

Sleep Softly
G D McKee

Sleep softly mother dear,
What caused the smile to pass across your face,
Was it a dream of happy days gone by
Or memory of a much beloved place.

Perhaps your thoughts had turned, as oft do mine
To childhood days, so full and free from care.
Was it a day when many years ago
You brushed and combed a mop of golden hair.

Did you feel small arms around your neck,
And hear small voices chattering on and on,
Or had you thought of days when first you met
The man who is the father of your son.

Had you recalled the days you danced till three,
The scent of honeysuckle in the air,
Or held your firstborn son upon your knee,
And marvelled as you watched his face so fair.

Sleep softly mother dear,
What caused the pain to pass across your face.
Was it the cruelty of youth,
When love and laughter could not find its place.

And did you think again of that sad day
When headstrong child now half turned into man,
Tore on his much beloved machine
Into the night, and crashed into a van.

Did you recall the days you felt despair
When nothing ever seemed to turn out right.
When fate and fortune seemed to be unfair,
And tossed you sleepless many a long long night.

Sleep softly mother dear,
What caused the joy to pass across your face.
Have you found peace once more,
And is the world again a happier place.
Do you feel small arms around your neck
And hear small voices chattering on and on,
Or had you thought of days when first you met
The child who is the daughter of your son.

Sleep, sleep softly, grandma dear.

Bradwell Woods 1959
Ian Hancock

Spring came in with welcome warmth
    to end long winter chill.
On our faces glowed the light so long denied;
    and in our hearts the urge to go
    along the narrow hedge-bound track
    up to the ridge-high woods.

The 'little wood' and farmhouse on our left,
and to the right the timeless meadowland,
on which for aeons past had grazed the countless beasts.

We knew the ridge was high and that below it
fell the steep descent to valley far beneath.
To our young eyes it seemed on endless drop
and fear replaced, but fleetingly, the joy that met our gaze.

For just ahead, in drifts of azure haze, bluebells lay,
indistinct in individuality,
until into their midst we set our way to go.

A breeze, playful and slight, moved the mass of blue,
as we crept nearer to each separate bloom,
internal space to view in so much vastness.

Into the depth of each bell bees were drawn,
sampling within the back-drawn lips
a heady mix of sun and procreation.

Close to the core of perpetuity our childlike innocence came -
unaware of Beauty's deeper truth.
For in our heads a fragrance strong banished all rational sense.

Here was our realm, our arcady,
among the grass, thick- scented, amply blue,
under a sky, high-arching far above,

beyond the young translucent leaves.
A simple creature free in Eden's light
could not have been more full of bliss than we.

We little knew that in our hands a rare inheritance lay.
For simple childish understanding had no force or power
to comprehend the richness of its essence.

Sages have warned: 'Never return to places
known in childhood; they will have changed'.
These words of wiser men I did refute
and truth revealed itself in starkness absolute.
For where once bloomed a source of great content
there now lay barren, wasted land, under an ever-changing
                                                    firmament

Our Holiday
Roseina Fox

Me my man, and eight weans, we went.
To Loch Lomond, to live in a tent.
Two motors it took to drive us all there,
we all arrived, without worry or care.
To live in a tent, I thought would be fun,
our first day, but no sign of sun.
Feeding time came, oh what a sight,
I'd to cook on my knees, from morning till night.
A two burner cooker, sitting on the floor,
I thought dear Lord, I can't take anymore.
The days that followed, were not quite the same,
we got some sun, but most of all rain.
Two deckchairs between us, were all we could take,
I thought good, no more housework, no beds for to make.
Kids away out with Dad, for a walk in the rain,
me left in the tent, with only one wein.
I thought I'll sit in my chair, and have a wee read,
I fell right through the thing, and battered my heed.
Five days left, with only one chair,
I thought dear Lord I can't take any mare.
But our dear sister Rita, she heard of our plight,
and phoned to our brother, that very same night.
She said, I've got some chairs, and a fold down table,
could you take them to Loch Lomond whenever you're able.
He drove down next day, with his wife and our mum,
It cheered up that day, I thought would be glum.
Life in the tent from then on, was quite fun,
a lot better than the day, it begun.
So roll on next year, when we'll all go once more,
to live in our tent, by the Loch Lomond shore.

Dallas
Gordon Macdiarmid

The Texas sun shone down upon that scene,
He handsome, young, she proud, and so serene,
A shot rang out, the message it had sent.
'Today, a bullet killed the President'.

He'd won the hearts of people everywhere,
By deed and word he'd shown them how to care,
Their faith they'd placed in all that he had said,
'Today, a bullet killed the world's hopes dead'.

A Negro woman breaks down in the street,
With her he'd fought, their prejudice to beat,
'Why must this be the way it has to end?'
'Today, a bullet killed the Negro's friend'.

She'd loved him, not as President, but man,
Done everything for him a woman can,
Now in her arms she held his broken head,
'Today, a bullet killed my husband dead'.

On two young hearts the fateful truth
must dawn,
No more they'll run to meet him 'cross the
lawn,
Thru' tear-stained eyes these simple
words are said,
'Today, a bullet killed my Daddy dead'.

The True Love Of My Life
Ann McKeag

Your silent presence touched me,
With energy unseen
To heighten all my senses
In the childhood of my teens

Every word you uttered
Every move you made
Was locked into my memory
To be replayed in my head

Did you know I watched you
As you stood upon the stairs
I was just a schoolgirl
But you were in my prayers

I prayed to God you'd like me
But how was I to know
That you were just as insecure
As I was long ago.

I didn't think you'd love me
So your words were lost, it's true
But now I know so differently
And there's nothing I can do

For you are married to another
And you're the kind of guy,
Who won't neglect your family
And here's the reason why

You are the other half of me
And everything you do
Is similar to all my deeds
For I am part of you

We do not need a clergyman,
To join us both together
For God did that when we were young
And we'll be one forever.

I now know that you loved me
As much as I loved you
I remember everything you said
And that what you said was true.

Your silent presence touches me
Although I'm not your wife
My darling you will always be
The true love of my life.

Love Hurts
Margaret Baxter

Now the pain the tears
 are in the air
Life's not the same
 it seems so unfair
Though you're not
 quite gone
I know it's ending
 I'm hurting, burning
Full of sorrow
 living only for tomorrow
Wanting to see
 your sweet face
Hoping to feel your
 warm embrace.
Oh my love have you
 truly gone
I sigh, I cry, I want
 to die
Without your love
 I can't go on.
Then I see you
 once again
The fire rekindles
 it's set alight
Warmth throughout
 our bodies flow
Passion has arisen
 our love's aglow
Maybe this time
 it will last forever
But just for now
 I don't want to know . . .

Regret
J Hazelwood

As I look into your wrinkled face
Imagine my heart, an empty space
Tear stained and desperate a silent plea
Mouth gaping wide silently
I realise now I should have bothered
To visit, to sit, to stay
It's easy now to see the mistakes
And the part I had to play
Guilt overwhelms me
The organ starts up and all that I can see
Is your coffin moving away
Into the fires of eternity

Lovers Always!
Valerie Powell-Jones

Their eyes first met one Irish Eve'
In a far-off place in the east,
And from the time their hands first touched
- They knew that love would reach.

As time passed by, their love grew strong
With a passion - full of fire!
Their needs, their love, their urgency
To feed each one's desire.

Their love was warm, - with tenderness,
Their friendship grew each day,
Their need to share and open hearts
Was what they had to say.

Their bodies 'ached', for every night
While they were far apart,
Their breasts were heavy, with such love
That was deepest in their hearts.

And when they touched, - with *searching* hands
Their feelings grew so deep,
It reached their hearts, it touched their souls
It left no time for sleep!

So, with a love so deep, so strong
They tried to live alone,
To give each other - what they felt
When they could be 'as-one'.

Alas, - with love, so intense
it sometimes has to part,
In a way that hurts 'two lovers'
To leave - an aching heart!

A heart that's torn ~ a heart that cries
In the darkest of the night,
To seek the peace within the soul
To bring the morning light.

And so, with time, which passes by,
When wounds are not so new,
These 'lovers', will keep in their hearts,
Their love ~ for always ~ true

Life In L A (Los Angeles)
Kenneth Waddington

My first time here, in 'Downtown L A'.
Everyone smiles, and says, 'Have a nice day',
But if you look behind this 'facade',
The smile has gone, the face is quite hard!
In this town, it's all 'Smog and Speed',
Everyone's rushing, forgetting the need,
For patience and such, to improve on it!
For here is a picture, if they could admit,
Maybe in time, L A will wake up,
See the true things in life, and drink from life's cup!
We don't have long here, so what time you have, use it,
Slow down, enjoy life, don't abuse it,
For soon you'll be gone, not leaving your mark,
Just imagine yourself, 'lost in the dark',
So for once in your life, be 'happy and gay',
And maybe life will improve, in 'Downtown L A'.

Giant Yellow Sunflower
Ashley Crabbe (8)

A lovely big sunflower
waiting to
be sown.
Then the day arrives.
He opens up the packet.
He rakes the warm soft soil.
He puts the seeds in a hole
and covers them up

July goes by
September comes round.
The garden shines
by the sunflower.

Reflections
C MacManus

I looked in the mirror
and what did I see
a reflection.
Could this really be me
the hair was silver, where it once was brown,
at the sides and on top of the crown
the lines on my face.
Could this really be
the reflection, yes it's really me
what can I do I cry in despair,
I know I'll colour my hair,
so out comes the bottle, it'll make me look young
wait 20 minutes and the hair will be done,
but to my dismay what did I see
a punk, as red as could be.
Its learnt me a lesson I can tell you
let nature take its course
else you'll look like this too.

Nature's Style
Jean Bowen

I went to work again this way,
The same road I follow every day.
But that moment seemed special somehow,
Opened my eyes and truly saw
Laid before me, I gazed in awe.
Nature's wardrobe again had wrought
The best in fashion that designers have sought.
Through the ages man has tried to emulate
The dress sense only she can create.
Colours of every hue and shade
Dancing before me as in a fashion parade.

Seasons come, and with them change
But Mama Nature knows just what to wear
Her robes are chosen with greatest care.
Mountains, hills, valleys and fields
Flowers, shrubs, grasses and trees.
An artist's palette just cannot contain
Enough colour that before me has lain.
Sometimes the vista takes my breath away
The scene will change again, next day.
Who knows what day I will face?
But always she calms me, with her grace.

Happy Days
Peggy Johnson

I'm gazing through an album,
of photos large and small
it's telling tales of a family,
who from babes, have grown quite tall.
A chalet by the seaside,
is where we took the shots.
Abersock was the place
we really love it lots.
Counting days to springtime,
summer and the fall,
when all the family gathered
it was better than a ball
and when the sun came beaming down,
red hot became the beach
burning all our tootsies
which made us -
dance the light fantastic
till the waters edge we'd reach.

The Spider
Irene Page

A spider is sitting in his web

He's got it anchored from tree to hedge

Although it is windy, and gets blown about

The rain pours down, there is no doubt

That the web is strong, and the spider is clever

For the way he has put his house together

The insects into the web, get blown you see

For the spider to tuck away, for breakfast

Dinner and tea

Swansea - Locked On . . .
Lincoln Allen

I came in to Swansea one bright sunny morning,
young eyes a shining and hair that was brown.
With a heart just as light as a breeze in a meadow,
I strode down the Strand in that dirty old town.

The sheepskins were stinking; the butter bins rancid
Oil drums all dented and soaking the ground,
Each railway arch rich with its scent of fish boxes
And other scents too in that dirty old town.

The old men depressed me . . . the women, no better
Their shawls looked so greasy and darkened their frowns.
I'd known only valleys and soft country places
I didn't feel right in that dirty old town.

At the gates of the coldstores, 'twas tho' I'd met Peter . . .
All dressed up in white from his feet to his crown
For he was the angel who pointed to heaven
When I needed a drink in that dirty old town.

I opened the bar door and trod on the sawdust,
It had me the feel of Elysiun Ground . . .
At the pumps stood a vision, her loveliness gleaming,
She lit up my life and that dirty old town.

Sixty years worth I've had of those bright sunny mornings
The smells and the rust and the greys and the browns
I could have made Sydney; Colombo or Rio . . .
But my heart locked me up in that dirty old town.

Springtime
Joseph Bottrell

The leaves are falling from the trees
Slowly floating in the autumn breeze
Frost and snow, will soon be here
Closing the end of another year
Days are short, but spring is near
Soon those dark days will disappear
Buds and bulbs, will be clearly seen
Followed by their leaves of green
Colourful flowers are soon on view
A beautiful array of red, white and blue
Birds will be singing, blue skies appear
Everyone's happy now that spring is here

The Streets Not Paved With Gold
Carol Mogford

London, London, your everything to me -
Your in my heart, and in my mind, your everything I see -
historic buildings everywhere towering so tall -
Gazing at them, from below, feeling lost and small -
In Portobello's famous market, there are bargains being sold.
But please don't listen, when they say, the streets are paved with
gold.

There's a force, that draws me, up there from afar.
Just like the three wisemen, who followed the bright star.
People from all over - come to visit this grand place
They are every culture, colour and race.
Dropouts, tramps and wino's clad in only rags
All their worldly goods, tied up in two bags
Begging on street corners, they take life's knocks so bold
None can tell them, the streets are paved with gold.
Victoria sits in marble supremely in her seat
Guarding the palace, motherhood at her feet
At Greenwich, you can board, the impressive Cutty Sark
Feed the birds, and sit peacefully, in St James Park -
The contrast of rich and poor, is not greater anywhere -
But there's always a con-man, lurking, like the fox inside his lair
Nelson's always watching, from his column up above
If he wasn't made of stone, he'd look at it with love
If he wasn't a statue, if he wasn't cold.
He'd take time to tell you, the streets not paved with gold.
But how I really love it, up there in the smoke
Catching rhyming slang, from all the cockney folk
I love the black taxi's and the red double decker bus

I love Oxford Street, at Christmas with the lights and all the fuss -
I love the Savoy and Ritz, and all the cafe bars -
The Royal Family, and all the superstars
Whenever, I feel lonely, depressed and oh so low -
London, good old London, is the place I want to go.
But if you want to go there, there's one thing that must be told.
Don't be fooled into thinking, that the streets are paved in gold.

An Ode To The Lowlands
Betty Melcafe

We came to Holland, really green.
A windmill we had never seen
And everywhere so bright and clean
Were we living in a dream?
And as for guilders quite unknown.
We couldn't even use the phone.

To cross the road, each time a thrill.
Those Dutch us Brits they want to kill
Each biker had it in his head
A point for every Brit found dead
White tiled tunnels oh so long
We hoped their roofs were good & strong.

For all that traffic up above
To fall upon us, they would love.
To the flower market then we sped.
In every form and colour spread.
Blooms we'd never seen before
Were laid before us on the floor

Then people charmed us with their smile,
They told us 'welcome, stay a while
So if we last 'til Saturday
A second visit we will pay.
And those who live to tell the tale,
Will safely on the Amstel sail,

When we return 'O land of song',
'Tis for the Netherlands we'll long,
There's a welcome in the hillsides.
There's a welcome in the vales,
But the welcome from quaint Volendam,
Could spin a windmill's sails'.

My Special Place
June Cullinane (62)

As I grow older,
My memory,
Can play tricks, I know,
But clear as day,
Is the way,
You held me in your arms,
The comfort I felt, the joy, the love,
Over the years.
Things have changed,
My hair, has grown grey,
But of the places,
That I have been,
That memory, is here to stay
That special place,
You led me to,
The heaven, that was you.

My Place
Belinda Hill-Upperton

I have a place I go to when life seems so bleak,
A place I know I will receive everything I seek.

I can change my mistakes, I can change my appearance,
I can change my life without interference.

I can be what I want, can go where I choose,
A winner in this game called life, no chance I'd ever loose.

In the place I visit there is nothing to cause fear,
I'll receive my heart's desire without shedding any tear's.

I'll find true love, my life long partner,
Our lives be full and rich with laughter.

In my place your never ill, no pain of broken bone's,
No last good-bye, no tears to cry beside a cold headstone.

No more sadness, no more sorrow,
For everyone a bright tomorrow.

Fields so green, a sky so blue, a sun that always shines,
I wish I could take everyone to this special place of mine.

I know it sounds impossible, amazing it may seem,
I promise you there's such a place but only in my dreams.

Childhood Memories
Lisa Horner

I look out of my bedroom window
At the fields and the wood
And I think back five years or more
When things were really good
The whole family would be in the garden
Shouting and playing games
Me and my brothers would argue
Because they called me names
Dad would be messing around
Making everyone smile
That's something I didn't do
For a very long while.
Dad passed away you see
This year will be five years
But I always love remembering
Because thinking of my Dad
Takes away all my fears.

Sea And Sand
Jennifer Whitehead

You were the pebble on the beach
I was the rough cold sea
You loved with such devotion
Always looking out for me

I was cold and reckless
Riding rough shod over you
I thought you'd always be there
Now what am I to do

I miss you, how I miss you girl
Since you walked into the sea
That day I finally wore you down
And you'd had enough of me

There's plenty of pebbles on the beach
Or so that's what they say
I know now I lost the most precious one
That day you went away

Love In Cheshire
Edward Francis

On the late night bus from Manchester,
An angel's hand in mine,
We travelled back to Stalybridge,
Under a spell divine.

Stalybridge -
Home of the girl I loved madly;
Stalybridge - gateway to paradise!
Now it's the town I think of most sadly;
After thirty-six years my heart pays the price.

Where is she now,
The goddess who lived there?
The angel who suddenly entered my life,
And as suddenly left it -
And left me bewildered:
Is she another man's much-cherished wife?

Lisa
Lily Hall

A blond whirlwind -
     came rushing through the door,
Shoes kicked off -
     coat thrown to the floor,
Toy box opened - a biscuit,
     a drink of juice.
Nursery school finished,
     she's on the loose,
A smile - a kiss,
     a great big hug,
A playful wrestle,
     on the fire side rug
Will I tidy up - waste of time,
     I have to concede.
My heart has a special place.
For this blonde whirlwind -
     seed of my seed.

A Gardener's Prayer
Isabel Wootten

Oh, Lord, our reservoir is low
At Pitsford. I expect you know
If you've been watching earth rotate.
Please, Lord, before it is too late,
Send soft, refreshing rain each night
But let the days be warm and bright.
The plants and trees we love to grow,
The grassy lawns we have to mow,
Your creatures, duck and trout and otter
All pray, please fill up Pitsford Water.

Worthy
Gwen Brown

When a robin, blackbird or a nightingale sing
I hear her voice in every note
A fox calls to his vixen or an owl hoots to his mate

I recall that evening of unforgettable bliss!
      If only I were worthy.

She is not beautiful or elegant, like the 'cats' that walk
                                    - the stage.
But comely, pleasant, with a heart of gold
She's kind to children, animals and such-like
Some seek her help, without a comforting word or hug.
      Yet, I feel so unworthy

We met in the superstore - she was on the till
Our eyes met and I dropped the bottle of juice
Our hands touched as we cleared up the mess
Useless - hopeless and awkward - that's me!
      I know I'm unworthy

At last, we were alone, one evening in the park
I cannot remember what she said but can recall
Her sweet voice, her gentle touch and the blue of her eyes
Birds sing, rainbows shone and heaven itself was nearly.
      I must be worthy now

One year has passed - our moments together are still divine
How it happened, we never knew but both concluded
The answer, so long awaited, was in our kiss
No words were spoken but so much was known
      I'm worthy - yes I'm worthy

Four years now, no happier couple could you find
Our little cottage, colourful garden, a swing, a slide
For our two little ones use, the elder is Worthy

His little sister is Hope, the moral here is, never give up
        Hope, to be worthy!

A Working Life
William Lea

A working life should be happy,
Each day a joy to be.
Willing, to help with others,
With the wheels of industry.
Whatever level of working, in office, or shop floor,
A laugh is all important,
Success will come for sure.

Skill and brains are needed,
Of that there is no doubt,
Within the wheels of industry,
To turn can't do without.
But a working life should be happy,
Something you must enjoy,
Not just a brief encounter,
For life you must employ.

So choose your right vocation,
Enjoy the wage you earn,
Be fair, both boss and employee,
A lesson for all to learn.

Summer Days
K S Welsh

Dawn . . . The lightness of the coming sun
      The mornings has broken, and just began.

Birds singing in the trees . . .
      Flowers buzzing with honey bee's.

Children playing in the sun,
      Laughing, joking, having fun.

Mum's inside cooking tea,
      For daddy, my brother herself and me.

Evening . . . The sun comes down, behind the tree's
      Dusk set's in with a calming breeze.

Stars twinkle in the night . . .
      Giving a glow, producing natural light.

That Was Then
Phil Sturgeon

The colours on the photograph may be fading
But the memories are somehow still there
For the time when we were together
Your angelic looks still remain
But how deceiving they were in the end
Why were you so shallow oh so superficial
When my feelings for you were for real
You deceived me into believing the baby was ours
How cruel could someone be
I wonder how many others have you left
Feeling like I did
Are you still the same now
As you were then those years ago
Broken promises and messed up heads
To the girl with the angelic looks
That I mistook for love
But that was then.

My Sleeping Child
Joyce Hammond

As I enter the room to wake him
And ruffle his tousled curls,
What a handsome sleeping lad he is
One of my two precious pearls.

He's too grown up for a kiss now,
He wouldn't like that at all.
Although sometimes the temptations great
To kiss him after all.

He's very deep in his slumber,
At last he's beginning to stir,
To waken to a fresh new day
Instead of dreaming of her.

What a heart-warming sight a sleeping child
Deep and so at peace,
It makes one feel so meek and mild
The love our heart's release.

Room With A View
Susan Boulter

There's a special room in my house where I often love to go
It always cheers me up whenever I feel low.
I look out through the window, to fields of vivid green,
The lambs are gently playing, it's such a pretty scene
This room is in my attic, and there so carefully stored,
Are cherished little memories, a really priceless hoard
These treasured little items, mean oh so much to me
They bring back all those years, when I was young and free
I sit in this room, with it's breathtaking view,
Lost in deep thought, of a life, I once knew.
High on a shelf, sits my old teddy bear,
It makes me feel happy, just knowing it's there.
An old babies shawl once so proudly worn
A photograph album now tattered and torn
Though the cushions are faded and almost threadbare
I contentedly sit, in my fireside chair.
I'll never get back those years, I once knew
But I'll always be glad, for my room with a view.

Faces And Places
R.Lucas

Now that you're older and have to go slow,
Do you yearn for the places of long, long ago?
Are there faces and places you never forget,
Places to which you can now never get?

Do you recall that as young girl or boy,
There were many things that gave you great joy?
Do you take yourself back to your birthplace or home,
And picture the places where you used to roam?

Did you live in thatched cottage with a white garden gate,
Or was it a house with the roof tiled in slate?
Could it be that your old home is no longer there,
Or sadly looking in need of repair?

Was your home in a village with pubs and a shop,
With a hall where they held a weekly hop?
Or did you live in a town and it your delight,
To go to the cinema every night?

Was there a place where you picked wild flowers,
Or a park where you liked to play football for hours?
Did you go looking for blackberries to eat,
Or prefer to play hopscotch in the street?

Did you have holidays by the sea,
Or visit grandmother for afternoon tea?
And was she Victorian, stern and severe,
Or very kind and rather a dear?

Were you clever at school or not very bright,
Struggling to get the arithmetic right?
And did you collect cigarette cards or stamps,
Studying them closely under oil lamps?

Was there a place where you curled up with a book,
Or did you help in the kitchen and learn how to cook?
Did you have on your birthday a special treat,
And look forward to that iced cake to eat?

Perhaps you feel sad and long for the place,
Where once you were happy and knew every face?
It wasn't all carefree, there must have been tears,
Just find the best bits and remember those years.

Parcels
Anna P Aldridge

Parcels are very mysterious things.
Everyone likes to receive them
They are tied up with various ribbons and
                                    strings
So well knotted that you just can't untie
                                    them.

There are small parcels, big parcels,
Square parcels, round parcels
Some that have beautiful paper wrapped
                                    around
Or they may be wrapped in ordinary paper
                                    brown

Some of the parcels you relieve might be
Shaped in a way that deceives you about
        The actual thing that's inside

But there is one thing you could not get
        Into a parcel, and that's a horse –

The kind of horse that you can ride

Step Back In Time
Sonia Coneye

Step back in time
I did by chance
And saw myself
At a glance
Memories of yesterday
Flooded my mind
As I walked streets
Hoping to find
The home that once
Was his and mine
Unable to stand
The test of time
Where children once
Played happy and safe
Now had the look
Of derelict disgrace
The birthplace
Of my babies born
Brought tears for
My heart was torn
Step back in time
I wouldn't advise
Memories are best left
If you are wise
Yesterday's gone
Along with rough seas
Tomorrow's the future
So let it be

My Basenji Boys
Tracey Norton

Thank-you boys for the ten
years you gave.
Thank-you also for the company
you gave.
'Do you remember our walks
come winter and summer sun?'
As your eyes shut the years
you gave me flashed by as if
a dream.
Dear Pasco I hope you're having
fun now you're with dear Danny?
The good Lord gave you both
to me, I was your keeper.
I long to be with you both,
We will be together one day.
The three of us can run along
the beach.
We can make foot-prints in
the sand.
'Remember me my Basenji Boys?'

The Gift Of Memories
E M Blanchard

Memories one never forgets
As I think of all that's past
The holiday's - and happy day's
And even bad one's too
But together - always together
We saw those bad day's through
A sadness now has come to me
And I am all alone
As I look across to speak to you
Then realise - you are not there

How I miss the talk's we had
The laughs - and the sharing too
It all adds up to a loving life
We shared so many years through
I remember the favourite walks we had
Strolling - hand in hand along the cliff top
Listening to the rush of the tide
Sweeping over the pebbles below
The smell of the sea, and the squeal of children
As they paddled, and played on the beach

I remember the picnic's we had on the island
Where you loved to fish from the rocks
And we would build a fire with drift wood
To boil water - and make tea sweet, and hot
I realise you had to leave me
As the pain was too much to bare
But you have left me the gift of memories
Memories, so sweet, so precious, and rare

My Valentine - To You
R Unwin

So - fourteen again,
Is it just a *game?*,
A date in a *year*,
Many love and yet fear.

A love - sincere,
A love - so *deep*,
My eyes do *weep*
Each night with *tear*.

I try my *best*,
But fail the *quest*,
Do what I *must*
To seek your *trust*.

But I dream '*on*'
And to aspire,
'Fore life *aeon*
To full *desire*.

Now dream *surpassed*,
Oh - joy to *last*,
Aft' love did *wane*
Re-born with *flame*.

My love for *you*,
Is with *delight*,
We are now *two*
For life and *flight*.

Home
Liz Hope

Days were sunnier,
Honey runnier,
Jokes were funnier -
In the place where I was born.

Fires seemed cosier,
Made cats dozier,
Cheeks turned rosier -
In the place that I came from.

The snow was whiter,
The moon shone brighter,
Burdens were lighter -
In that magic place called 'home'.

Bluer, greener, crisper, cleaner,
Better, longer, neater, stronger -
Ev'rything was so much clearer,
Sharper, nearer, warmer, dearer
In the place that was my home.

One Life Span
W E D Edwards

When a new born baby comes into the world,
With a smile so big and sweet.
They clench their tiny hands,
And curl up their tiny feet.
They make a lot of washing,
And turn your life upside down.
When they are keeping you up at night,
You feel you want to shout and frown.

Yet they are so small and bonny,
Unique in just every way.
You just have to love them dearly,
Because they only want to play.
The years will go so quickly,
Treasure those moments while you can.
For soon they will be adults,
And start another life span.

Fields Of Stones
James Devon

Walking through the fields of stones
Where are you now Jimmy Jones
All that's left is earth and bone
Just a memory carved in stone
A woman cries by an open grave
Breaks down and screams for her Dave
Died so soon in his short life
Left two children and a wife
Here lies an old friend of mine
Ran out of luck and out of time
Maybe we'll meet again some day
Floating through the milky way
Little Emma didn't know shy
three years old and born to die
All that's left is her toys
Jesus loves the girls and boys
The cruellest hurt must be when
Parents bury there own children
I wish I had a single pound
For every tear that's touched this ground
life is short but shorter for some
Sooner or later our kingdom will come
In our time we get one chance
So dance when you can dance
For today I'm going home
'Till the next time here I roam
One day not too far away
Here I'll come and here I'll stay . . .

Our Over 60s Club
Mabel Harrington

I hope you like our posh new cups
Which you all helped to buy
In just six weeks we had enough
Our wants to satisfy

We set ourselves a target
A hundred quid to find
Fifty brand new china cups
Was what we had in mind

Every week we had two tables
To put unwanted on
Some made cakes and apple pies
Some the humble scone

We had jumpers, skirts and night-dresses
Handbags, belts and shoes
Such a good assortment
For everyone to choose

We had lovely mats in crochet
And bric-a-brac as well
And some gave generous donations
Our meagre funds to swell

There was lots of to and froing
As the money just rolled in
It really was encouraging
To hear it rattling in my tin

There was a saying years ago
So I've heard my mother quote
You exchange old rags for gooseberries
When you were really broke

My Home

Lorna June Burdon

My home is a very special place,
Now retired, I relax and enjoy the quieter days,
Many jobs to be done, but with no routine to follow
What isn't done today, can be done tomorrow,
Home is a favourite chair, beside the fire
With feet up, a cup of tea, the TV on for an hour.
My home is a dwelling of comfort and security
A special place which I hold the key.
It is also a base where the family gather
Where troubles are shared, and we help each other,
My home is full of memories, which I treasure
With sad times, happy times, tears and laughter
There has been many changes over the years
Being widowed twice has been hard to bear.
Home is a special place for children too,
Growing up with love, to see them through
Their teenage years, then married life
With homes of their own, and children to guide
I stand at my door looking into the garden
Each day, with pleasure, I see the flowers blossom.
When on holiday or a day trip to town,
I always look forward to coming home.

Paradise Lost
Sharon Goldsmith

A place of my own
To be all alone
No people, no phone
It's heaven.

Some peace and some quiet
My own preferred diet
Why don't you all try it?
It's paradise.

Away from the rush
No hurry, no push
There's plenty of hush
It's peaceful.

Time stands quite still
Get up at your will
Time in abundance to fill
It's slowly.

No company . . . no talk
Alone you will walk
There's no other folk
It's boring!

Your Place

Charles Alun Jones

We've come to see your spirit free,
Here the place. You would like to be.
Here, you can dance in the seas breeze,
Be content, relax, feel at ease.
Here, like a seagull you can soar into the sky,
Float with the waves into the shore.
Not worry about the where's of why,

But feel at peace for evermore
Here strong with lighthouse you will stay.
In our hearts and memories never to go away.
And in time we will come here to your place,
We will feel through the wind, your kiss on our face,
Feel happy in thoughts and, memories of you,
For you were a very special person Ness that's true.
You gave us love, understanding and new ways of life
to see.
So with sweet thoughts let your spirit be free.

Return To Childhood Haunts
Jean Allen

Have you ever returned
To a place you used to know,
A part of your happy childhood,
Perhaps many years ago?

I did such a thing
Only the other day,
To where my Grandmother lived,
With whom I would often stay.

I stood by her cottage
Of white and black
And there in the quiet
Memories came back.

I went for a walk
Along the way,
Where as children
We used to play.

As I trod the quiet footpath
On that sunny day,
I could feel recent tensions
Slipping away.

When I reached the place
Where the orchard had been,
There were no trees now,
Just grass turning green.

How we'd dodge the wasps around a tree
As each picked a juicy plum,
Holding it so carefully
Between fore-finger and thumb!

There are now modern dwellings
Where the old farm-house had stood,
With their patio windows
And bright painted wood.

As I continued, I was grateful
That in these days of change,
Of progress and development,
This footpath with its kissing gates remains.

Finally, I reach the church yard,
My nostalgic journey's end,
And there, in the enveloping calm,
My Grandparents' grave I tend.

Thoughts On Moving To Llanddower-S W Wales
Dorothy Moody

Listen to the whisper of the water by the willow,
Listen to the buzzing of the ever busy bee.
Listen to the lowing of the cattle in the meadow,
Listen to the country and relax along with me.

See the sweeping swallows bringing promise of the springtime,
See the modest primrose and the violet so shy,
See the little calves, the new born lambs upon the hillside,
See the country, see the beauty, let the world go by.

Come now, leave the city life, the hustle and the stresses,
Here the days pass peacefully, there's time to stand and stare,
Watch the changing seasons, see the earth don many dressers,
Here, for city dwellers, is the answer to a prayer.

The Visit
Marjorie L Nuttall

I come to England every spring
And as the plane floats down
My happy heart begins to sing
At sight of countryside and town,
For this is the land of my birth.
The Country that adopted me
Can boast a massive girth.
A landscape that is wild and free,
Trees that dwarf our oaks and elms,
Plains that make our meadows small,
And greatness too within the realms
Of its colossal waterfall.
Natures bounty breeds contempt
For though I love the Country of my choice
I find the miles of forest too unkempt
It's in the miniature of England I rejoice.
When at the end of spring I've had my fill
Of pleasure from its rosy flowering ribes.
Its slender tulips, sunburst daffodils
And new sweet smell of nature on the breeze,
I can return with memories to treasure
Whilst round me a much wider screen unfolds
Bringing a different kind of pleasure
In its myriads of yellows, greens and golds
For autumn is this Country's time of splendour
With Maple trees bedecked in flaming red
And as I dwell on this with thoughts so tender
I know its to the best of both worlds I am wed.

The Price

Christina Ecclestone

Loving Jesus, you have bought us
With a price so great, so free
Giving your life as a ransom
Dying there on Calvary

Oh, the cruel death you suffered
Oh the pain, the blood, the tears
Yet the last words that you uttered
Hath remained throughout the years

Wondrous love, none can compare it
Boundless grace if you believe
Come to me, my love I give you
Free to all, who will receive

Hollingsworth Court, Our Home
Nora McGuire

Let it rain - let it blow
Does it matter if there's snow?
We are here - in our home
And we're very safe you know.

We have friends all around
From the top floor to the ground
We have Jackie - we have Joan
There is little need to moan.

Though we miss all those who've gone
They are *replaced* - one by one
And their memories never fade
Although new friends we've made

It is sad that some are poorly
And yet we know that, surely.
When we get to hear them
We send a gift to cheer them

Though we used to like a game
Now, it isn't quite the same
We prefer entertainment more
And of artists we've had quite a store

And although such times are past
We like to *be* here to the last
And no matter where we roam
We *love* Hollingsworth, our home.

Loneliness
Sabrina Coelho (16)

Loneliness embraces my broken heart
of which you were so great a part
its been three months since that fateful day
when they came and took your soul away

Together we made a beautiful home
each room filled with your bright happiness
but now I am here all alone
with memories of you, I can only reminisce

Everywhere reminds me of the life we built
I long for your hugs and tender kiss
yet the blossomed flower of our love now wilts
oh those unforgettable days and nights I miss.

Only A Glimpse
Rosemary McEntee

The day breaks, I wake, I think of you
Wash, have breakfast, still thinking of you
Hurry through my chores
And when my work is done,
I'll be at your graveside at the
Setting of the sun.
So much to tell you.
So much to say.
Of all the things that you have
Missed in just one day.

Maybe you heard the blackbirds
Singing, having fun
Maybe you saw the children go
Through the school gate one by one
And was it you that dried
My eyes mid morning when I cried
And did you pat my hand and say
I am with you you'll be OK

So tonight as I sit at your graveside
I really just come to say
Thank you for being with me
And sharing in my day.

Conscientious
Harold Lamb

What's happening at the present day?
There are so many places in disarray,
Which were once so orderly and neat,
Now crude writing and paint adorn the walls,
In every town and street.

Litter, has now become a reality,
I am amazed at some people's mentality,
Observing them every night or day,
Dropping their rubbish on the ground,
With a litter bin an arms length away.

Someday will everyone agree,
Instead of saying, 'it doesn't concern me',
When something beautiful has been defaced,
Anything refined seems to be the target
And sometimes cannot be replaced.

Is it any wonder in this day and age,
Why complacent people fly into a rage,
When seeing the damage being done,
Every day to their environment,
Guilty ones say, 'They did it just for fun'.

Prayer
Ann Deacon

Father in the quiet of this eventide
Let me rest in peace by your side
Teach me to be wise and understand
To see good in those of every land.

Bless those who dwell in the darkness of mind
That thy light of love, they too shall find
Grant them courage to face each day
And faith, to help them on the way.

Let love and peace with us abide
Let not colour nor creed divide
Show us the way, to walk without fear
Knowing that thou ain't ever near.

Lord teach us to love and pray
Thru grace, you will light the way
                                        Amen

My Favourite Place
Alun Harries

Now where would I like most to be?
In my bed it has been said,
I like to spend most of my time,
Now tell me is that such a crime?
But no or yes, I must confess,
When I awake my hair's a mess,
My eyes are soggy, my brain is groggy,
I have no wish to walk the doggy.
Through closed eyes I fantasize,
Am I dreaming, is someone screaming?
The man's not singing, the clock's not ringing.
So let me slumber, let me be,
Although I wouldn't say no to a cup of tea,
And a slice of toast,
Two things that I like most,
When I realise, it's time to rise,
From 'My Favourite Place'.

A Nanny's Life
Hayley Gillson

I'd start off the day in the usual way
I would sit and watch the children laugh and play
To them it's their future
To me it's just another day.
They'd all gather round me and
Seem to know my name
They would call me 'Mary Poppins'
And then ask me to play their game.

I've loved and cared for babies, kids and brats
From dirty bottoms to snotty noses
To tickles on their backs.
From first words to first steps
I've been there all the way
These children shouldn't forget me
I've been there every day.

I was there to kiss them goodnight
And there when they opened their eyes
All the hugs and kisses they gave me
Never came as a surprise,
For that is their love from them to me
And that made me very happy
As you can see.

Of all the children wherever they may be
Do you think they will ever remember me?
For I am long forgotten
Probably slipped from their minds,
It's hard for me to say
They've probably left me behind
Or would they remember me for the fun things we used to do,
And if my name was mentioned, would they reply 'who'?

These children were part of my life
I think of them every day
For I remember all their names and faces
As if it were yesterday.
I gave these children everything
But love most of all.

I should pat myself on the back
And could stand up tall
I should be proud of myself for a job so well done
I've had a good time and also lots of fun
But all I can do is sit down and cry
Continually asking myself why?
These tears I cry are tears of pain
As I look at their pictures and think Gosh!
Will I ever see them again.

For now it is time to think it all out
To have my own children and stop messing about
I need my own family to love and to hold
I will always be there
And that they must be told.
They will always be mine
There's no saying goodbye
But I will never forget the memories
Of my past gone by.

For Molly
M Wimpenny

Fifty? What's fifty? A time in our lives
We've grown up together, we're mothers, we're wives
We've seen good and bad times, with hopes joy and fears
And even in dark days, we've laughed through our tears.
We've planned for our old age, what fun it will be
We'll buy a wee cottage and we'll live by the sea.
We'll relive our young days, - and folks will just smile
As we hitch up our skirts and paddle awhile.

Sixty? What's sixty? Now, you'll never know
You've been taken from us and we miss you so.
There's an ache in our hearts when we mention your name
And somehow we'll never again be the same.
Still, we've picked up the pieces and life will go on -
But when we walk on a beach or throw bread to a swan
You'll be right there with us, just as before
And you'll live on in our memories for ever more.

A Visit To A Special Place
G Allen

I visit rarely now the place of my birth
and youth.
The returning always excites me as no
other journey does.
I walk down the road so often Trod
in other times to where the house once
stood.
I stand and look for yesterday and listen
hard to hear a voice or sound to bridge
my absent years, to make me feel
home again, to give joy to that part
of me that never left.

I look through yesterdays eyes for
yesterdays people, but no one knows
today's me and I'm the stranger in
a very familiar place.

Child's Delight
Bernadette Francis

Swinging up high on my swing
I can hear the sweet birds sing,
I can hear the bees a buzzing as
they fly from flower to flower, I can
hear the church bells ring and the
choir when they sing. I swing
so high hour after hour, I can see
the old church tower. I can feel
the warm shining sun and see the
new spring lambs as they run.
Up here on high I can see you
when you walk by. I don't forget to
wave to me. I'll have one more swing,
then I'll go in for my tea.

My Room
Maude Pearl

My room is a room where I go
But, I am never alone
There is always somebody with me
But they never say a word.
My room is a room where I go
To get away from people
But when I get there
There is always someone there.
My room is full of people
Every time that I am there
There is seldom a single moment
When my room is totally bare.
My room is full of people
But I don't really care
They don't bring me comfort, joy or pain
They can't there only in my brain.
My room is always empty
But I think it's full
Of people that I'd like to know
But I never will.
My room is always empty
My head is full of thoughts
I wish I never had them
But I always will.
My room is my dream
It's where I want to be
If I can't be there
I don't want to be anywhere.
My room is my room
But no ordinary room
My room is full of gloom
But never happiness.

My room is my room
But it will always be
My room full of gloom
Until I grow up and leave my room

Untitled
Deborah R Moar

A feeling of sadness wells up inside
as I think of the feelings I often try to hide
not wanting to impose on the happiness you have found
my feelings are stuck, going round and round.
Gradually boring a hole somewhere inside
the pain comes and goes like the ebb of a tide
the pain is not sharp like the blade of a knife
but rather a dull ache sobering my life
causing me to realise how much I cared
when so many perfect times with you I shared
it's a frightening thought the effect you've had
I'm still not sure whether it's good or bad
but even after hurting more than I thought I could bare
I still wish we had more moments to share
but someday I realise I have to let go
and accept my love for you I simply cannot show
I hope it's better to have gone through the fall
than to never have had the chance to know you at all

My Mother
Divy Macleod

My mum raised 10 children over 45 years,
And still can manage to hide the tears,
She made our clothes when we were small,
Comforted us when oft we'd fall,
Washed our clothes all by hand,
All evening at the sink she'd stand,
Got up at nights when we were sick,
When often cuddles did the trick,
Made our breakfast, dinner, tea.
Told us stories one, two, three.
Taught us what was right from wrong
When we felt weak she'd make us strong.
She had many hard ships to make ends meet
And so looked forward to any treat.

Kirbymisperton & My Granny Foxton
V M Catlin

We would catch the bus in the market place and it took
                              the Pickering Rd.
Past farms and pretty cottages and fields of harvest gold
We got off at the Beansheef stop and walked up the lane
Taking a pound of butchers sausages, we were going to
                              see Granny again
My Granny Foxton was a small woman, rosy
                              cheeked and neat.
With a shawl around her shoulders and skirts down
                              to her feet.
She did all her cooking on a range which she kept
                              black-leaded bright
And she trimmed and cleaned her oil lamps, which
                              were her only light.
Granny was a good cook, she made lovely cakes and bread
She could skin a rabbit in a minute and make
                              brawn from a pigs head.
She did her washing in a dolly tub and used
                              a great big mangle
Which nearly seemed as big as her and I often turned
                              the handle.
We went errands to the village shop which sold
                              just everything,
From groceries and candles, to buckets, brooms and
                              string.
Sometimes when we were playing, she would call to me,
To take my Granddad's bread and cheese and
                              billy-can of tea,
Over the fields to where he was working for these were
                              the years of war,
And young and old turned out to help, as they had
                              done before.
And when his day was over he would get down the
                              domino box

And we would play dominoes with him while Grandma
                                        knitted socks.
These were for the forces, round and round the
                                        needles flew.
She never sat with idle hands, she always found
                                        something to do.
And if you stepped into her pantry, the shelves were
                                        always full
Of home-made jam & chutney and bottled pears and plums
Now they have built Flamingo Land and traffic rushes
                                        up the lane
And when they've spent the day there, it all rushes
                                        back again.
I've been back many times since then, I stand out in the lane
And if I close my eyes real tight, I can see her there again
She's pottering round the garden, she's making
                                        Granddad's tea.
I wish that I had told her then how much she
                                        meant to me
I'll store the memories and I know I'll go
                                        again.
            Down Kirbymisperton Lane

Future Past
Jamie S Newland

The moment of clarity faded like charity does.
Sometimes . . .
I open one eye,
And I stare at the moon through the hole in the clouds,
And memories of you come flooding down.
Priceless jewels,
That sparkle deep in my memory crown.
And there's a hurt in my soul
That's more than just pain,
When I think that I'll never ever
Hold you again.

The Mirror
Ian Lansley

Look into the mirror and what do you see?
A reflection of what is or may be.
Go closer, go on don't be afraid
Nothing will harm you it's only glass behind a shade.
You can see the whole picture of you and 'something'
But what is that something?
Is it *you* and the beauty within.

The Country Man
Rosemary C Whatling

Springer spaniel close at heel,
brown eyes filled with such appeal.
Watching as master collects his ferrets
putting on his coat, whatever merits.
Off they tramp, man and dog,
whatever season, rain or fog.
Over fields of buttercup yellow
or dark brown earth dry and fallow.
Hedge rows alive with chirping birds,
or spars at time before rebirth.
He loves the feel of the falling rain
beating down as he treads the lane.
Looking for the rainbow high,
shining through the stormy sky.
Summer brings the sky larks song
as she soars above, all day long.
Never tiring of each new season,
he loves them all, and with good reason.
Nature who is Mother Earth,
sings her song for all she's worth.

Dedicated to my brother
Tony for his 60th birthday.

The Countryside
James Brailsford

I awake to a brand new morning,
it's the beginning of another spring.
The leaves on the trees, dance for me,
the birds are happy to sing.

After breakfast, I go for a walk,
along the country lane, we need to share,
I am peaceful and content in the countryside
but sad that you're not there.

The countryside knows, of the promises we made,
of the many dreams that, now, can't come true.
The flowers you used to touch seem lonely,
as lonely as I am for you.

I will always stay in the countryside,
this is where I want to be.
It holds the one wish, I keep,
that you, will come back to me.

A Meadow At Dawn
W Warne

Dawn is breaking
Mist is in the air
Gossamer cobwebs everywhere
Flowers and grass are wet with dew
Birds are singing their dawn chorus too
In the distance a pheasant calls
Doves are cooing.
Creatures waking from their sleep
Foraging for things to eat.
Like the hedgehog and the mole
A fox is on the prowl
Rabbits peering from their den
Daring to come out again
Dawn has broken
The world is awakening
A slight breeze- stirs the trees
The mist has cleared
The sun comes up
A new day has begun.

A Day At The Seaside
S M Harris

A day at the sea-side lifts one's soul,
Travelling light, a flask and ham roll.
Refreshing cool breezes from the sea,
The cry of the gulls, flying high and free.

Relaxing in deckchair, admiring the view,
Enjoying the brass band, trombonists on cue.
Watching children building castles to the sky,
Groups of trotting donkeys taking riders by.

Feeling, underneath your feet, the warmth of golden sand,
Searching in the rocks for crabs, fishing net in hand.
Seeing steamers chugging past out in the deep blue sea,
Where are they all going, which destination quay?

Men with hankies tied round heads, trousers rolled to knee,
Feet as red as lobsters, paddling in the sea.
Playing cricket on the beach, seems like a good game,
Now the tide is coming in, calls for careful aim.

Strolling out along the Prom, taking in the air,
Maybe later in the day, a visit to the fair.
Whether it be Barry Island, or even Langland Bay,
A visit to the sea-side, takes all your cares away.

My Jesus
Jean Thornton

My Jesus I love you,
OI saviour divine,
For ever your with me
Till the end of my time.

My Jesus, my saviour,
We never will part,
For ever you'll stay
Right here in my heart.

My Jesus, my saviour,
My Lord and my friend
My blessed redeemer
For ever Amen.

Friends
Doris Irene Radford

The pleasure of their company,
The comfort that they bring,
To know, that you can talk,
              and share.
Life's many pleasant things
And when, in time of sadness.
Who better to help cheer.
Than the friend who helps by
Words, and looks and deeds.

Fun On The Farm
Robert G Picot

My Uncle's farm, Highclere Thame,
Is really a cool place to be.
There're chickens to chase and sheep to shoo,
It's such fun for boys like me.

When cousins are there it's far too much,
And the fun too great to bear.
We collect ducks eggs, tease the dogs,
And drink loads of ginger beer.

Auntie Di bakes cake to eat,
She really is ever so kind.
And Uncle Tone takes us down the field,
To see what we can find.

There's mushrooms to mash, apples to munch,
And Poppy to pat, push and pull.
A stream to splash, trees to climb,
But the tractor is best of all.

When it's time for home, Dad's had enough,
And Mummy's gone round the bend.
We all feel sad and make a fuss,
Cos we don't want the fun to end.

But sheep must sleep, ducks must doze,
And dogs in their basket rest.
Chickens high roost from foxes feast,
While children at home are blessed.

Country Memories
J Mary Dobbinson

Apple blossom falling gently on my face,
Sets me to recalling another time and place,
Daffodils are dancing, new born lambs are prancing.
A meadow sweet with clover and we know that winters over.
As April showers fall, a rainbow bright will form,
And down a lovely country lane a primrose we will find again.
Then as we stroll through golden corn,
The lovely summer days are born,
Picnics, sea and golden sand
Memories fill my day dreams and tears fall on my hand,
Then the scent of new mown hay,
As harvesting fills every day,
Giggles and laughter fill the air.
As a ride on the hayrick we all share.
Michaelmas fair and country dancing
Harvest moon and light romancing
And come Septembers misty morn,
We gather mushrooms after dawn.
And as the evening shadows fall
An oil lamp lights the hay filled stall,
The gentle cow will now be milked.
And we will have a sweet warm drink.
The falling leaves of autumn, a blue pellucid sky,
It seems that summers left us, she didn't say goodbye,
The farmhouse kitchen warm and bright.
New baked bread and what a sight,
Jams and pickles, bottled fruit, in the larder we store our loot,
Jack Frosts icy fingers touch the window pane.
The magic sparkle of his hand turns everything to wonderland
And winters here again,
Our sledge goes skimming o'er a meadow,
Once bright with flowers now white with snow,
Church bells ringing, choirs singing.
Stars are shining on still night air.
The cold of winter grips the farm,

But inside we are trying hard.
To wait - with all anticipation,
A Christmas full of expectation,
The joys and love that Christmas brings.
Will last us through till spring time sings.

Going To The Day Centre
Rose E Selby

I go to the centre -
Each day of the week.
I see lots of people,
To many I speak.
We talk of the weather,
And things we have done.
We speak of our families,
The daughters and sons
The friends that we have,
And just how we feel.
Oh! isn't it lovely?
And all of it's real!
I'm sure there are others,
Just wishing that they -
Could go to the centre -
Like me, every day!
Long live the centre!
Don't take it away -
Cos where would I go -
And spend every day?

Flowers In The Park
J Bushell

We went to London on a special day.
The people were gathered with nothing to say.
The tears rolled down - not a sound to be heard,
but the flutter of wings from a few passing birds.
The flowers lay like a colourful lake,
each with a message the heart will break.
The coffin goes by with the tears in our eye
'We love you Diana' cries a voice close by.
Into the park a service to watch.
A place on the grass was the nearest we got.
An English rose was Elton's song
in our hearts we know she is gone
we walked to the Palace - the crowds were still there,
laying more flowers and a few teddy bears.
The world joined our sorrow in London today
the funeral of Diana has now passed away.

My Special Place
Sylvia Derbyshire

It was a dark and windy beach, somewhere
On the coast.
Where I stood and waited, for the man
I loved the most,
It was war-time, and St Valentine's Day, many
Years ago.
I waited fearfully, my heart was
Beating so,
Suddenly I heard the sound of a
Soldiers feet,
As he came towards me, my heart
Just missed a beat,
We ran towards each other, and
Hugged and kissed awhile,
Then he put a ring upon my finger,
With a gentle smile,
That was over fifty years ago, but
I would like you to know,
He is still my husband, and I
still love him so.

Rosie

Clive Chandler

There's a special lady in my life
I can not do without
Cos if I did not have her
I would be but nowt

In the morning she helps me dress
And helps me with my socks
And when my hair grows back
She will brush my golden locks

She helps me in the garden
Keeping down the weeds
And if she's got a moment
Then she is sowing seeds

She keeps on going all the day
And says everything is fine
But the best thing of all is
I know that she is mine

She really takes good care of me
I could not ask for more
Or maybe she could fan me
While I lay on the floor

Thank you for looking after me
And helping me with life
Yes this is you Rosie
My loving, loving wife

I don't know how to put to words
Just how much I love you
Except to say Rosie
I do, I do, I do

Thanks mate
Your loving tubby hubby

My Haven
Barbara Symons

You are my own wee haven
My place where I can rest
Where love is unconditional
And care is of the best
When toil and care becomes too much
With you I always get in touch,
And come to stay till worries are gone.

Then rested - calm - refreshed
      Go home

For Yvonne

The Holiday
Lynne Done

The holiday is booked now,
There's nothing more to pay.
They're going for the week -
Not an outing for the day.
The journey's end is Cornwall,
The sun is shining down
The car is packed full to the roof,
They're on the roads from Town.
Soon they're in the country,
Driving carefully down the lanes
Passing fields of playful horses -
With swishing tails and manes.
Then starts the moans and questions
The laughter and the sighs,
But suddenly as if by magic
The sea is before their eyes!
Up goes a roar of happiness
The journey has been worth it
They all get out to stretch their legs,
The cottage looks just perfect.
But wait! what is that up above?
The clouds are gathering by -
It looks like rain or maybe thunder
It makes you want to cry!
But that's the British holiday
And what a joy it is
To dart between the showers
It adds that extra fizz!

Thirty Years On
Sue Albinson

The old house is closed,
and boarded up, oh what I'd
do if I had some luck.

The day the bailiffs ousted
us out, as kids we felt
helpless no doubt.

The monkey house too has
fallen to pray, it was flattened
and removed to clear the way.

Bogurt Hole Clough is exactly
the same, the old trees we
swung on, still remain.

Thoughts and feelings come
flooding back, as my brother
and I remember and laugh.

Our wives follow on and
start to smile, as much as
to say, what does that house hide.

We felt today the old
mans boot, as we went
back to our old roots.

Monsall still stands where mam
strived hard, dressed in blue
she saw her job through.

For just a day Rochdale
Road let our old
memories and whispers unfold.

A Walk In The Woods
Jean Warboys

I love to go walking in woods nearby,
In the clear fresh air where the pigeons fly.
On muddy tracks through towering trees
Where the branches creak in the gentle breeze;
Some are clad in an ivy wrapping,
Far above the woodpeckers are tapping
Sunbeams dapple the woodland trail
Through the high tree trunks and leafy dale.
A splash of yellow from catkins in bloom,
The primroses keep their own little room.
Two muntjacs are grazing the nearby crop
With a watchful eye, before they hop
Over the ditch scurrying and lobbing
Bouncing along with their white tails bobbing
Into thickest bush and darkest space
Where they have their secret hiding place.
Animal footprints criss-cross the track
Where fox and deer have been there and back.
There's so much to discover in this wild wood,
As a home for our wild-life for years it has stood.

Our Place
E Woodsmith

Didn't take us long to find the place
Down the winding country lane.
Under three large oak trees it stood.
It's 'only claim to fame'!
On a grey and misty morn
The trees - oh, so forlorn.
Certainly didn't look at all inviting
But - then the sun came out.
And I knew without a doubt.
This is where I would be living.
And we did - for ten years.
It was quite enchanting.
That little house among the trees.
The place I left my heart in.

Tender Touch
Wendy Mahoney

Your warm and tender touch
is felt my all, this day
and in my quietest moments
in my heart, for you I pray
I pray that God will bless you
and lift you high above
and cradle you in his tender arms
with such soft and caring love
I pray that he will lift you
and hold you in his arms
and soothe away your problems
with his soft and gentle palms
I pray that he will give you
strength for each new day
for you to continue caring
in your soft and gentle way
I thank my God ~ I met you
and spoke to you; each time
for that very soft sweet smile
was heaven sent to shine

Looking Upwards
Monica Butterworth

Mid December - the churchyard cold and bleak.
The chill wind whistling round the old, high gravestones.
Has life gone from here? not quite.
A few mortals scurry by
Sombre, drab. Some in a hurry, some aimlessly;
Men, women, and children,
Their eyes downcast, their thoughts elsewhere.
The weariness of life - and death-is all pervading.

But these unseeing eyes have missed so much.
In the corner of the churchyard is a cherry tree,
No ordinary tree, but one in full pink blossom
In this cold, dark month.
Who casts their eye upwards as they pass
To catch its sheer beauty, shape and colour
Against the pale blue of the cold winter sky?

No one - not even a child -
What a pity, what a loss.
What joy there is just for the looking.
The promise of spring in winter,
And the promise renewed each year.
Surely someone must notice?

Yes! one person saw it, suddenly as
She turned past the old yew.
Her eyes lit up, her pace slowed,
She paused, drank in the beauty.
Her weariness was shed suddenly
And quietly, like the sepals of those pink blossoms.
For her, at least, life had a new meaning.

My Love
M E Lawrence

My love believe me when I say,
I love you so in every way,
I could not face another day
Without you my love.

My love beside me always stay
At night beside me, always lay
Promise me mine you will always stay
My own true love.

As I clasp your body close to
Mine
I drink your kisses sweet like wine
I can't believe your really mine
My love, my sweet, sweet, love.

For My love
Anton Steffen

My special place
    is being on cloud 9
wrapped around in my girl friend's arms
    just knowing that she loves me
there's no other place
    that I would rather be
resting my head on her shoulder
    while she rests her head on mine
just the thought of being with her
    oh she makes me feel so alive
a woman full of mystery
    and caring with her love
sometimes, I think
    she is a angel
sent to me from above
    she turns the rain into laughter
and the winter into spring
    she turns the spring into summer
oh she means everything to me
    this woman fills my heart with happiness
like I have never known
    to me she is very special
and I would like the world to know
    for now I have found a perfect love
so rare during the mists of time
    for she is so very precious
and one day she will be mine.

Dedicated to Alison Rose

Favourite Place
Phyllis O'Connell (Hampson)

With no disrespect for my late husband and all the rest of the family
My favourite place would be with my mother you see
We do so miss her
Everyone who knew her would agree
      No matter how busy she was you knew
      She always was there for you
Why am I living so long sometimes she would say
How do you know?
Well it was not because she sat around
Mum was always on the 'go'
      Our mother had such a sweet voice
      Sang while she did her chores
      Did not scream, knew all the words
      In fact at 95
      We were just glad she had her faculties and was alive
Dad gassed in first world war
His sister Caroline used to say mums cooking kept him going
He worked hard
Sarah Georgina (mum) certainly could not have done more
      Queuing, cooking, working during second war
      Seemed to come natural
      We came home to wonderful meals regularly
      She would never say if she was tired
      Mum managed the rationing so well
You realise things as you get older and you go away
It's not because people have a lot
That they know what they are doing
That is why every detail is with me to this day
      Personal letters also say a great deal
      My husband wrote about her
      She sang, she cooked and always had a smile
      And a cheerful word
      So intelligent, much faith, honesty and good living
      And a Giver
      A Survivor

Spring
Beryl Manning

Spring is here
Can you feel it.
See it all around,
Apple blossom on the trees
Gently swaying in the breeze
Birds singing!
Happy is the sound.
Birds nesting at their ease
Bulbs appearing everywhere
Their little green stalks
Looking like statues on parade,
All the trees looking green,
Fish in the pond now can be seen!
Smell the fresh air after the first fall of rain!
Oh it's lovely!
It's spring again!

Places
Sharon Helliwell

'Home is where the heart is!'
Anywhere in spring,
I think is the thing,
Every where's home,
When you hear nature sing,
The fruits of her labour, summer will bring!

The beginning of budding romances,
Even animals are taking their chances,
Some strong commitments
Some just fancies,
As autumn approaches and winter dances.

When winter arrives and it's plain to see,
Saying 'I love you'
Knowing 'You love me'
Is really and truly,
'Home for me!'
We are all natures creatures,
              Deemed to be!

In The Meadows
L Montaque

In the meadows,
I stroll and play,
until the skies
become dark and grey.
When I have had enough
I run home to safety.
Then start a new day
in the meadows again.

This Special Place
Margaret Bernard

There is a place
Where big birds land
      with relish so grand
      on golden sand
      and triumphant stand
      to greet a welcome hand
In this joyful, special place.

There is a place
Where big birds fly
      way up on high
      in a silver sky
      and loved ones cry
      to wave their last goodbye
In this sorrowful, special place.

Garngad
Catherine Alderdice

There's many a time my memory returns
To a place I used to live
I was just a youngster at the time
To return, there's nothing I wouldn't give

A very happy childhood
Game's in a concrete yard
Sunny days and little friends
A happy smile was not hard

There also was some mischief
And disobeying mum
I'd wander off to the canal
Big brother for me would come

Sent on errands to the shop
And told to come straight home
The lure of chums and sand-pit
Temptation too much to overcome

Alas, they're gone those happy times
They'll never return, it's sad
They even changed the place's name
The place I call Garngad

To Charles
Joan Cox

Who is to comfort me,
   now you're gone?
Who will hold me in his arms
   and stroke my hair?
Who will put the world
   to rights
And set the tone which
   gives me hope,
Who will gaze at me
   with eyes of love
And murmur in the
   morning
'How have you slept'
And touch my face in
   wonder and in joy,
That loving me is what
   you do.
Who, who, who?

Summertime
Russell Thompson

Oh for the summertime, how I long
For the warmth and the flowers, the birds on song
Whistling aloud a happy little tune
Dancing aloft in the month of June.
Fresh cut grass, it smells so well
In the distance, the sound of wedding bells.
Long cold drinks, we stand in the shade
Whilst the children, barefoot, in the stream they wade.
Foreign holidays and a room with a view
From the streets below, the aroma of a barbecue.
Out with a ball in the local park.
Longer days and no early dark.
Laughter and ribbing from everyone you meet
All around there's parties in the street.
Soon to be gone, as here summer doesn't last so long
Back to work then for everyone
Next is golden autumn in all its glory
Soon to be here but that's another story
Some prefer spring, winter even with all that white
But me, I prefer summertime and all seems right
Oh for the summertime, how I long
Must wait for the next one now, cause this one's gone.

Two Lives, Two Loves
Sandra Heath

I've left part of my heart,
Far far away.
And in this place it will always stay.
I've memories deeply rooted in my mind
And they are of the happiest kind,
Of New Zealand a life I once knew,
Where as a child I grew.
I lived there for quite a while
And life brought me many a smile.
But two decades and it was time to go,
From that place I'd come to know.
So here I am in England
And now this is my home.
For from your roots, you seldom really roam.
My heart though is forever torn,
Between the place I hold dear,
And the place I was born.

Stepfather
Joy Walker

Only through my eyes can you see,
Just how much you really mean to me,
The special relationship that we share,
And how much for each other we care
It means more to me than you'll ever know
The love and respect I hope I show
Through all the good and the bad
Just remember 'I love you Dad'

The Mean Machine
Ann Beard

I'm just waiting for you at your club,
Yes they have my relation at your local pub.
A machine with fascinating flashing lights,
So you stand in front of me with my delights!

Listen to your money fall and rattle in,
Then you press the button to make me spin.
But I'm rigged so you think you're nearly there,
Oops! I will not pay out till your pockets bare!

My owner empties me and gosh he is rich,
When you loose you just think I'm the bitch!
You're the one who has thrown their money away,
Sorry only a fool will stand there and play!

Afraid there's always someone who thinks he'll win,
That's why others, just stand watch and grin!
But think they should feel sorry when you're broke,
No, they just think you've got past a joke!

Now you're hooked, so borrow to feed the machine,
Wake up, can't you see, this machine is mean!
So you're a born loser and now you're in debt,
At least I've got your money, I've won my bet!

Sweet Rose
Alan Reid

Sweet rose of you I often dream
Each year grow with tenderness
Beside that little shady stream
My love for you I must confess
A thing of beauty natures child
Your all alone in that dear place
With deep repose so meek and mild
To gaze upon your sun-drenched face
When days grow short and summers gone
I stand beside that flower and cry
When winters frosty days return
I watch you fade away and die
But in my heart I know some day
Sweet Rose that you will come again
And I will smile again and say
Hello again to you dear friend

Is There A Place?
Georgina Sim

There's a place in my heart
For my mother too be
A thing filled with love that runs true and free.

There's a place in my heart
For my father too be
No one can fill it
It's got to be he

There's a place for my husband
That's close to me
Hugged in his arms that's where to be

There's a place in my heart for Robbie my son
And also for Kevin my youngest one

Is there a place for violence and crime
No not in my heart there isn't the time

Is there a place where each one could reach
For love and some kindness and peace they would teach

Not in this place can our kids play out side
Something is out there evil it hides

Not in this place can we live for tomorrow
Knowing what's in the papers nothing but sorrow

Is this a place where our children should be
I wish I could say yes but its not to me.

Nostalgia (Old Glasgow)
Maud Hamilton

Houses were small, families large
Dad's went out working, Mum was in charge
Coal bunkers in the hall, toilets on the stair
Everything spotless, each does his share
Stairs brushed daily, pipe clayed and sparkling white
The old valley close was a welcoming sight
Not much money for sweets and treats
Going to the pictures in the cheapest seats
Good clothes on Sunday's for going to church
or visiting relatives, keeping in touch
Sunday school parties, Sunday school trips
Sails 'Doon the Watter' in paddle wheel ships

These are the things, we remember with pride
We forget all the bad things, Nostalgia can't hide
Tenements dingy, grey and gritty, where workers used to stay
Dirty courtyards, not so pretty, where children had to play
Clarty pavements, filthy streets
Pawn shops, where the two streets meet
No DSS to help those in need
Food eaten to stay alive, not just for greed
No NHS to look after our health
Treatment received according to wealth
Welfare clothes everyone knew
Children without a sole to their shoe
People working from morning to night
To earn meagre wages, to exist was a fight

Many years have passed since then, life for most people is better
The rent of a one time 'But and Ben', we pay to post a letter
We've machines for this, machines for that
The once humble tenement is now a luxury flat
No more smog from open fires, we all have central heating
Hoovers clean our carpets, no need for all that beating
Clothes are washed and dried, without a lot of strife

Hi-fi's, TV's video's, brighten up our life
The car, we use to get around, we don't often walk
TV is the major thing, people seldom talk
We use the phone to call our friends, this way we keep in touch
To get around to visiting, would trouble us too much
I don't know if we're happier, living life at this pace
I only know it's getting rare, to see a smiling face

A True Friend
Thomas Murray

When the sun goes down at night
And the daytime will disappear
I say goodnight to my true love
With a smile and a single tear.

She will come to me in the morning
And I will be smiling again
If it wasn't for her tenderness
Then I would surely go insane.

I haven't been well for a number of years
I have really been going dizzy
But my loved one has really made sure
That I am always kept busy.

She is my soul of inspiration
My very own guiding light
I must keep my wits about me
For I must try, with all my might.

She takes me to our special place
Once there, we can both unwind
We take in the beautiful scenery
And forget everything else in mind.

Before you know it, the time has gone
And so we set off for home
No more time to dilly-dally
And no more time to roam.

And so the night comes round again
I must still get on with my life
There would be nothing to get on with
If it had not been for . . . my wife . . .

Infidelity
J Fitzpatrick

Darling I love you with all my heart
I hope and I prey we will never part
I will never give up on my quest for you
My love is honest, pure and true.
These words come from my heart and not my head
Rather than harm you I'd sooner be dead.
I quote note from poems and prose
You will always be my beautiful rose.
Although things haven't always been right
I'll fight for you with all of my might
Not with anger fists or sword
But with my heart! I give my word
These are things at present I cannot alter
But my love for you will never falter.
One day I hope we shall walk on the sand
And once again you will take my hand
Perhaps we will be able to forget the past
We will find a future and a love that will last
We can learn a lesson from our mistakes
Too many things for granted we take
A wild bird should not be kept
Since you left my life
I have never slept
My heart is heavy
My soul is so troubled
Let's go look to the grey mare's tail
Where the wild water bubbled!
We'll gaze in the pool at the waterfall
We'll start afresh on a new path
And forget one and all.

Water
Charlotte Razay (9)

Think of calm quiet water
Lovely and soothing
Dip your finger in and out
Spreads a ripple.

Now think of a world with no water
No people, plants, animals and no water,
Cracks in the earth, nothing left.

Think of the ocean
Big giant waves,
Dolphins swimming in the sea
Just like it should be.

Springtime
Clare Moore

Cycle rides beneath blue skies,
Bird song heard in hedgerows green,
Meadow adorned with bluebells
A gentle breeze whispers through the new grown leaves
Springtime

A Letter To My Love
Babs

I remember the night we met
our life together was set
We had our sad and happy times
But I was yours and you were mine

The kids have all left our home
And you have left me all alone
I loved you in life and I love you still
And I will love you forever, or 'til

'Mr Sandman' was our song
And you loved the one called 'Sway'
But 'Honey' we'll meet again someday
And go on loving in the same old way

We will never ever have to part
And that will heal my broken heart
You said you'd never leave me
But that was not to be
The Lord came down and took you away
But we'll be together one lovely day

You were my husband and I loved you so
So why, oh why did you have to go?
You left me without even saying goodbye
And left me alone with tears in my eyes
I'll never forget you, you know that is true
Until the day I'm in heaven with you.

Llandudno Sands
Ellen Green Ashley

A group of ten, they waited by the pier.
The price chalked on a board stuck in the sand
drew hordes of children clutching this amount
in hot and sticky hands. 'Now, form a queue',
the man called out and all of us obeyed.
Each donkey had its name across its brow,
tattooed in white on chestnut leather straps.
My fingers crossed that 'Bonnie' would be mine -
the smallest one, with tufted coat, long ears
that I could tell my secrets to; a mane
for stroking (or for hanging on!); sad eyes
of velvet brown that blinkers could not hide.
I watched, impatient, as they trudged along
towards the ice-cream van, before the turn
which brought them back to where I stood in line.

My turn, at last, as hoisted skywards by
the strong brown arms into the seat, I felt
the smooth and shiny saddle stiff beneath
my short bare legs, and heard the creak of strap -
on-strap, the jingle of the harness bells.
Adjusted stirrups reached my ankles, not
my feet as I had hoped - but dare not say.
The man with leather face held out a hand
and put my sixpence in his leather bag.
A wave to parents standing by, the crack
of cane upon the donkey's rump, before
we made our way across the sands. Too soon,
it seemed, we reached the van and circled round
to face the pier. (A trot could be a treat
for one or two, but made my bottom sore
though I held on and tried to 'bounce' as I
had seen the riding classes do). How long
ago it all seems now, but childhood sights
and sounds & smells return as we grow old.

Whispers To Dad
Val Rigby

Wherever you roam in my garden, I'll be with you.
The fragrance of your rose tells me you're there.
Although I can't see you, the essence of your being
Wafts round me, cushioning me, showing that you care.

As long as I have my garden you will always be on my mind,
I will always keep a bower quiet for us.
Never will you fade into nothingness while your rose feeds on the
earth
As I find solace when, with you, I can unwind.

The Loss
William Brand

The sound of laughter fills
The air.
Kiddie's play around your chair
A simple tune would play away
To help you cope with every day
Alas the music fades away
So all we do is kneel and pray
But memories are so divine
Until our arms again
Entwine

A Small Holder's Life
F J Simpson

My wife bore three children
and I was the father
but sometimes I've thought and felt I would rather
have been one of the kids
and not just the father

And thinking back now, although we were strict
we never corrected them all with a stick
'the run of the mill' to coin a phase
was given them all, though they never did laze.

A small bit of garden was given to one and a shed
to make a few things that came into their head
a hammer and nails and odd bits of wood
surprising the things that came out and so should

As for brains they weren't lacking, though teaching was scarce
as I had a farm to establish, or else!
my wife had to slave to see to us all
no neighbours nearby, no help could she call.

Today they have settled in various ways
though sometimes I look back and long for the days
when we were all young and happiness hovered
but where would we all be if I had not bothered?

Christmas On The Long Row
Veronica Taylor

It seems like only yesterday,
When mum, dad, my brother and me,
Used to go to auntie May's and uncle Albert's,
At Christmas for our tea.
We'd sit round the kitchen table
And enjoy a lovely spread.
There was a large black fire place
With an oven on the side
And the smell of home made bread.
I can remember opening our Christmas present's
And the time my brother got a gun,
He squirted cold water on uncle's bald head
But it was taken in good fun.
I remember the warm glow from the fire
As it flickered across the room,
The chimes of the grandfather clock
As it struck on the hour
And Christmas ending too soon
If I could choose to step back in time,
I know that's where I'd go.
To auntie May's and uncle Albert's,
Known as, the long row.

Home

Eileen M Taylor

Home is where the heart is
so long as you are there,
and when I see the moonlight
reflected in your hair.
Starlight dancing in your eyes,
soft wind that stirs the trees,
as long as we're together
my world is made of these.
The open road my heaven,
the brown earth for my bed,
with heather for a pillow
where I can rest my head.
Or in a country garden,
somewhere the wild bee sips,
where we can live and I can
taste the honey on your lips.
My idea of heaven is
just knowing that you care;
then my home is where my heart is
so long as you are there.

The Mendip Hills
Olive Thompson

I know a wood on the Mendip Hills,
Where wild anemones grow,
They flower early in spring;
They look like lace amongst the heather,
Where deer and rabbits graze together,
I take my children there in half term,
To see this beautiful sight;
They say they can hear the fairies sing,
As they dance around the lacy ring,
If we go there again at the end of the term,
The flowers will be over but the leaves remain,
And we know that they will flower again,
At Easter time next year.

Untitled
Diane Tamminen

This is my place, I always knew it would be there,
I felt its gentle breezes dancing through my hair,
It took my breath away, and drew me back again
Helpless as a child,
So green, so rugged uncontrolled, yet wild,
This is my place, I did not ask a part of me to stay,
or let it drift into my mind, while taking part
In every day,
It calls me back, and time, and time again, I go
But not against my will, I love it so.

Special Place
P M H Wood

Our wonderful special place of yesteryear
Although the name now has changed,
It still holds memories that are dear
Pictures in our minds have not aged.
Sweetly scented long days and nights,
Peace, warmth and the beautiful sights.

The artful brightly painted flowers
And tall elegant palms gently swaying,
Green parrots winging above for hours.
Sun from the blue yonder never straying;
The sparkling sea casting its spells
Upon golden sands decorated with shells.

Many stars filled the Navy night skies
A multitude of jewels shining down.
At dawn the fine mist upward flies,
A spiders web hanging like a gown,
The birds begin their sweet song
All to our special place belong.

Isles Of Beauty
Anita Slattery

No matter where in the world you roam,
These isles are your heritage and home,
They have enchanting nature . . .
All made by the wondrous creator:

England, Ireland, Scotland and Wales,
Places where you where born,
Keep their picture ever in your mind,
Regardless what other places you find:

Many leave these shores . . . 'Never to return',
Their homeland forever to say goodbye . . .
Yet there may come a time when they ask themselves . . . 'why'?
And deep down long to be back again,
With anguish and pain:

Children of today . . .
No matter what blood is in your veins,
All have a heritage . . . and there is always a welcome home,
In that place that is truly yours:

If ever you get that chance to return,
Your heart with pride will burn,
With that feeling to stay,
And not like your parents . . . ever again stray:

In Memory Of Richard - My Dear Husband 1935-1987

Heather Moore

You lived for fifty years and two
  Of these, twenty six I spent with you
We loved, we laughed and cried
  For each other, we would have died

This 'thing' growing in your head
  A tumour was the word 'they' said
An 'op,' five hours and you'd be fine
  Little did I know - I was 'buying' time

With tubes so many, you smiled at me
  Our fingers entwined gallantly
I whispered 'together we'll see this through'
  But wondered - how long have I got you?

Who was it who had stood six feet tall
  With fine physique and now -
A crumbling heap - stumbling on your feet
  Blind and deaf - no more to speak
Nappy clad - spoon fed - no hair, quite bald
  From chemotherapy I'm told

For one year I've nursed you - was I wrong?
  I wrap my arms around your body cold
Forgive me darling - goodbye, God bless and thanks
  Now my tears gush forth - no more do I have to hold
You are at rest - one of God's best.

In The Highlands Again
Paul Andrews

There's a gentle breeze blowin' on the loch,
And the sun is beating down upon the glen,
There is no place I know that can compare,
To being back in the highlands once again with you,
To be back in the highlands once again.

There's an eagle flying high above the trees,
Soaring wild and free and calling on the wind,
And the freedom of the air will send him home,
To be back in the highlands once again with you,
To be back in the highlands once again.

Tha mi an dochas gum bi turas math againn,
's chi sinn an iolair, na beanntan is an gleann,
Far am bheil na feidm a' chruinneachadh air an froaich,
'Sann anns a' ghaidhealtachd a'rithist bithidh sinn,
'Sann anns a' ghaidhealtachd a'rithist bithidh sinn.

(Gaelic translation:
I hope that the journey will be good for us
and we'll see the eagle, the mountains and the glen,
where the deer are gathering on the heather,
in the highlands again we will be
in the highlands again we will be).

The Hustle And Bustle Of Christmas
Mary Brown

For a woman nearing Christmas day, is such a hectic time.
So I thought, why don't I try, to put it into rhyme.
We must do this, we must do that, there's such a lot to do,
We think we'll never make it, but, somehow we always do.

All the fare is brought, and is ready to bake
The turkey is ordered, and the icing's on the cake
We've trimmed the windows, doors, ceiling and walls
With tinsel, chandeliers, and frosted snowballs.

We've bought ourselves a new party dress to wear
Carefully wrapped up the presents we bought with such care
Some in pretty paper, with coloured bows and tags
Others are sealed tightly in Christmas scene bags,

We have wrote out the cards for family and friends,
Wishing them seasons greetings and our love to them send,
Better make sure there's no one we've missed,
Now where on earth did I put my list.

The tree now it's decorated is a sight to behold
Right on the top is a shining star of gold
The tinsel glitters, and the lights twinkle so bright
With pretty bows and baubles and snowflakes so white.

The children carol singing at the door sound so sweet
We listen a while before we give them a treat,
Their little faces so rosy, from the cold frosty night
Thank you and merry Christmas they shout with delight.

When Christmas Eve comes and we have done all our tasks
At last we can relax with a drink
When up pipes hubby, did you send to so-n-so he asks
I did I reply (or did I?) I'm too tired to think

Home
Myra Walker

I love being indoors
On a treacherous night
When the violent storm
Is reaching its height

The wind comes tearing
Across the field
But my wee house
Will not yield

Hard and driven
The rain doth batter
But I'm inside
It doesn't matter

I feel so cosy
The curtains drawn
I know I'm safe
'Til the morn.

Thank you Lord
For my haven here
It is to me
So very dear.

Bob's Meadow
J A Rogers

There's a meadow,
Green and fair -
Bob and I
Spent hours there.
   Buttercups
   And daisies grew -
   Horses shared
   The meadow too.
There's a rabbit
Over there -
Bob couldn't catch it,
He didn't care!
   Grandchildren came
   They too had fun -
   Round the meadow
   In the sun!
Seasons drifted
In and out -
And as I walked
Bob chased about.
   Frost on the grass
   Sometimes snow -
   Up to the meadow
   We'd always go.
The meadow now
Seems dark and cold -
Bob and I
Have both grown old.
   Bob can't see
   The meadow now -
   But I'll have
   Memories - so many
   Memories . . .

Filey Brigg
A G Moore

Filey Brigg juts out of the sea
It is a special place, for me.
'Tis here the sea may gently swirl,
Or rage about like a rebellious girl;
Where seals may bask in the sun,
Swim in the sea and have fun;
Where the rocks emerge and disappear
As the tide flows in and out, here.
'Tis here that people paint or fish,
Walk, watch birds or make a wish.
Why is this place so special to me?
It's here my loved one's ashes be,
Thrown into the wind and out to sea,
A final request from him to me.

The Adventures Of Me And My Cherry Pie Cosmos
Laura Honeyman

Falling off my cherry pie cosmos,
I landed with a marshmallow bump in a town,
Where the roads were made of lines of cough candy,
With fudge toffee houses all around.
A strawberry-cream robin hopped past my feet,
And I watched it fly up to a candy floss tree,
Where it twirped with its family of strawberry cream robins,
In a nest made of twiglets and raspberries.
The tree stood tall in a garden of jelly,
Where a gingerbread woman was hanging out clothes,
Her children were playing with their caramel kitten,
Her husband; watering plants with a liquorice hose.
Suddenly, I heard a large crunch in front,
A cream cracker car was sounding its horn,
I jumped out of the way onto the coconut pavement,
And knocked over a post box made of corn.
Well the townsfolk were not too impressed with this,
For I had ruined a part of their precious town,
I heard someone shout 'call the polo police',
I knew they were going to hunt me down.
Out the corner of my eye, I saw an escape,
My cherry pie cosmos was floating nearby,
I jumped on it hurriedly and it whisked me off,
For further adventures past the blueberry sky.